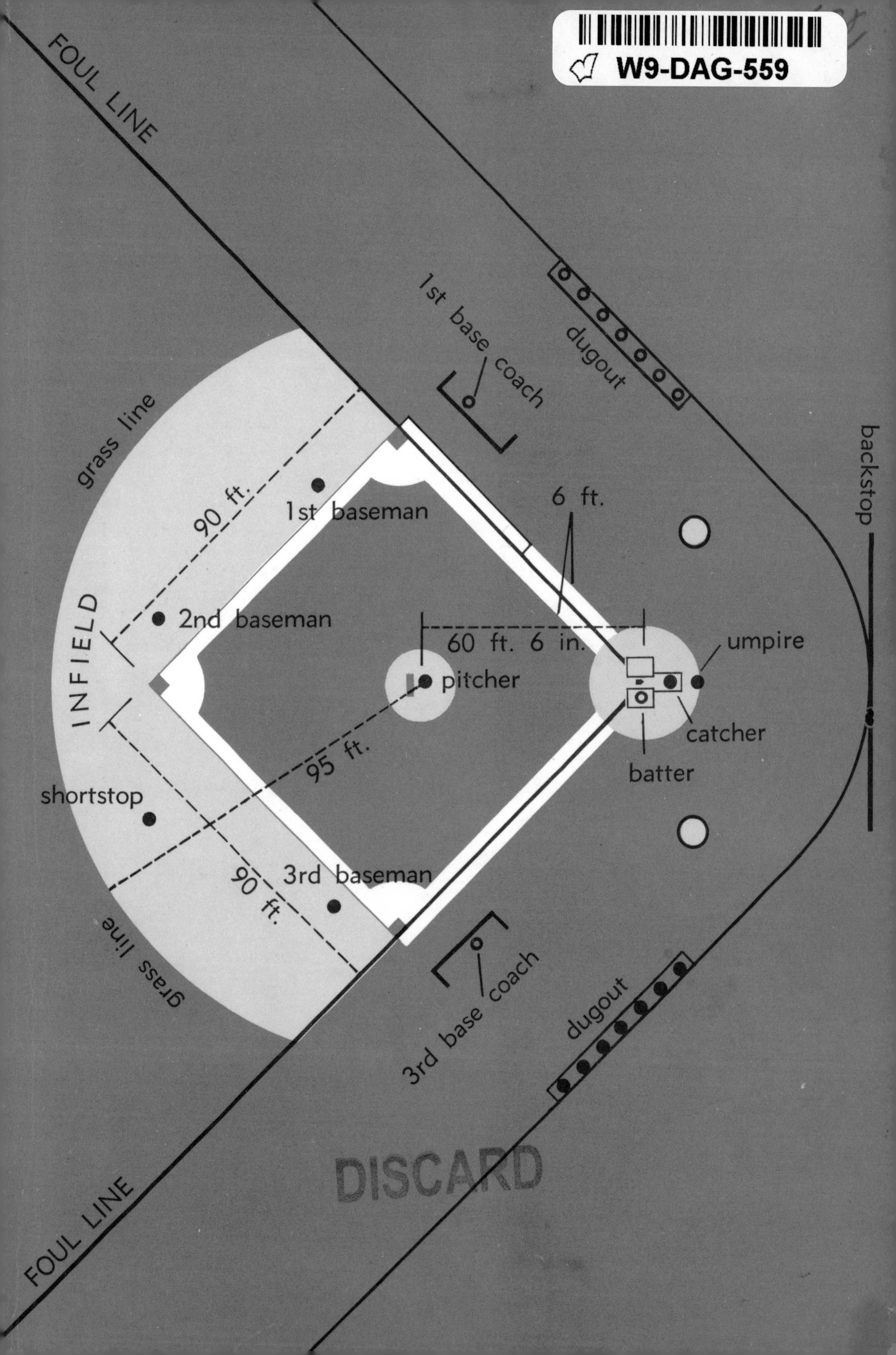

FOUL LINE

1st base coach

dugout

backstop

grass line

90 ft.

1st baseman

6 ft.

INFIELD

2nd baseman

60 ft. 6 in.

umpire

pitcher

catcher

95 ft.

batter

shortstop

90 ft.

3rd baseman

grass line

3rd base coach

dugout

FOUL LINE

DISCARD

BABE RUTH
SULTAN OF SWAT

★ ★ ★ ★ ★ ★ ★ ★ ★ ★ ★

BY CHARLES SPAIN VERRAL

GARRARD PUBLISHING COMPANY
CHAMPAIGN, ILLINOIS

43485

To Evan Stoliar

Sports Consultant:
COLONEL RED REEDER
Former Member of the West Point Coaching Staff
and Special Assistant to the West Point
Director of Athletics

Acknowledgment:

State Senator Jimmy Walker's speech on pages 74 and 75 is
from *Beau James* by Gene Fowler © 1949 by Gene Fowler.
Reproduced by permission of The Viking Press, Inc.

Photo credits:

Brown Brothers: pp. 3, 38 (top), 66, 72 (top and bottom right),
    82 (top), jacket
Culver Pictures: p. 72 (bottom left)
National Baseball Hall of Fame and Museum: pp. 14, 23
Underwood & Underwood: pp. 1, 38 (bottom), 47 (top), 52
United Press International: pp. 4, 10, 17, 28, 47 (bottom),
    63, 69, 79 (both), 82 (bottom), 84-85, 88, 91, 92

Library of Congress Cataloging in Publication Data

Verral, Charles Spain.
    Babe Ruth, Sultan of Swat.

    1. Ruth, George Herman, 1895-1948— Juvenile
literature. 2. Baseball— Juvenile literature.
I. Title.
GV865.R8V47   796.357'092'4 [B]   75-38825
ISBN 0-8116-6679-4

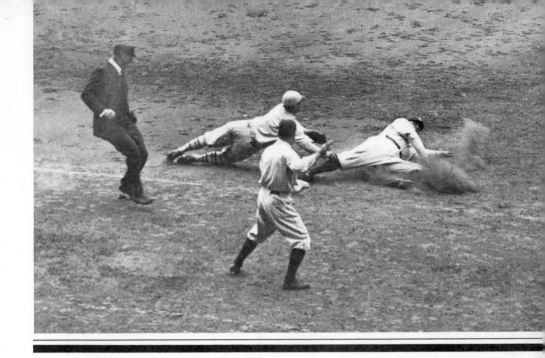

Contents

1. The Called Shot

Babe Ruth, the famous home-run king, picked up his favorite bat and stepped out of the New York Yankees' dugout. The stands in Wrigley Field, Chicago, were jammed with people. When the Chicago fans saw Babe Ruth, they let loose a storm of boos.

"Don't let it get you, Babe," the Yankee manager told his star player. "They're trying to make you lose your temper so you'll strike out."

Babe Ruth shrugged. "Let them yell," he said. "It won't bother me."

It was Saturday, October 1. The third
game of the 1932 World Series was being
played between the New York Yankees and
the Chicago Cubs. The two teams didn't like
each other. The Series so far had been a
stormy one. The Yankees had won the first
two games in New York. The Chicago Cubs
were anxious to win this third game on
their home grounds. The score at the start
of the fifth inning was tied, 4-4.

The Yankee lead-off batter grounded out.
Babe Ruth was up next. As he walked to
home plate, the yelling from the stands got
louder. The reserve Cub players stood at the
front of their dugout and joined in the
booing.

Babe Ruth paid no attention. The big
left-hander dug his spikes into the dirt of
the batter's box. He held his heavy 44-ounce
bat ready just above his left shoulder. He
looked out at Charlie Root, the Cub pitcher.

6

"Strike him out, Charlie!" a Cub player shouted.

The right-handed Chicago pitcher went into his windup. He threw. The ball cut cleanly across the middle of the plate. Babe Ruth did not try to hit it. Before the umpire could make his call, Babe Ruth yelled, "Strike one!"

He held up one finger of his right hand for everybody to see.

"Give the big clown another strike, Charlie!" came a shout.

On his second pitch Charlie Root threw wide for a ball.

"Let him have it, Charlie!" shrieked a fan. "He can't hit anything."

Again Charlie Root pitched. The ball zipped through the strike zone, bullet-fast. Once again Babe Ruth failed to swing.

"Strike two!" Babe Ruth bawled out. He raised two fingers.

"Put this one over, Charlie!" another fan yelled.

The Chicago pitcher played it safe. He threw wide. The count was now two balls, two strikes.

Babe Ruth glanced over at the Chicago dugout, where the reserve players were still jeering. He looked up at the noisy grandstand with its rows of unfriendly faces. Then Babe Ruth did something that people would never forget.

He raised his bat and pointed it in the direction of the center-field bleachers. He held the bat outstretched for a long moment until everybody knew what he meant. He was signaling that he would hit the next pitched ball for a home run. Not only that. He would hit the ball so it would land where he pointed.

Babe's gesture angered the crowd. The Yankee had to be struck out.

The ball park grew quiet as the Chicago pitcher fingered the ball. All eyes were on the big man at home plate and his big bat. In came the pitch, fast and knee-high.

Babe Ruth waited a split second, his brown eyes on the ball. Then, he took a step forward and swung the bat with all his might. There was a sharp *crack* as bat and ball met.

A groan came from the Chicago fans. The ball streaked high above the infield. It cleared the outfield. It disappeared into the center-field bleachers exactly where Babe Ruth had pointed.

Babe Ruth trotted to first base, then to second, then to third. A broad smile was on his full-moon face. Suddenly from the Chicago crowd that had been so against him came a faint cheer. It grew into a roar as more and more people joined in. They were no longer just Chicago Cub fans. They were

It's a run! Babe Ruth crosses home plate.

baseball fans and good sports. They knew that they had seen a great athlete perform a once-in-a-lifetime feat.

As Babe Ruth headed for home plate, he glanced up at the cheering people who were suddenly his friends. He took off his cap and waved it to them.

The Yankees won the game, 7-5. Afterward a reporter spoke to Babe Ruth.

"That took cool nerve, Babe," the newspaperman said. "What if you had swung at that last pitch and missed?"

Babe smiled. "I never thought of that," he said. "I guess I was sure I could do it."

The New York Yankees went on to win the 1932 world's championship in four straight games. It was a great victory.

But even more unforgettable was Babe Ruth's fifth-inning home run. Forever afterward it was known in baseball history as the "called-shot" homer.

2. Early Days

Babe Ruth had not always been as happy and sure of himself as he was on that day in the 1932 World Series. When he was a small boy, he was often lonely and frightened.

Babe Ruth's real name was George Herman Ruth. He was born in Baltimore, Maryland, on February 6, 1895. He was the oldest of eight children. Only George and a sister, Mamie, five years younger, lived beyond babyhood.

George's father ran a tavern in a poor section of the city, close to the waterfront. Its customers were mainly sailors and dock workers. Their language and habits were rough. Drunken fights often broke out in the tavern's bar.

George and his family lived in rooms over the tavern. His mother worked long tiring hours, waiting on tables and helping her husband at the bar. Her health was poor, her nerves worn, and she often took to her bed. She hadn't the strength or patience to deal with her active young son.

George received even less attention from his father. He was a tough, short-tempered man. There was no real family life for George. In later years he was to write, "I hardly knew my parents."

From the time he was six, George played in the streets at all hours. He was big for his age and at seven could pass for nine or ten. He seldom went to school. Instead he spent his time with a gang of tough boys, all much older. They taught George to

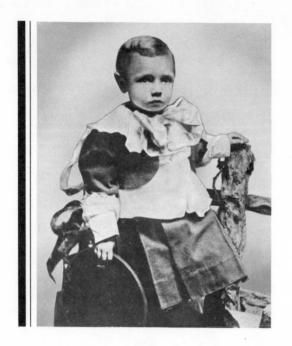

When this picture was taken, three-year-old George was a model child.

swear and to fight, to snatch candy from open store fronts and to steal money from his parents. The gang was often in trouble with the law.

One night a rock was thrown through a store window. Cigarettes and chewing gum were taken. Two of George's friends were arrested. The next day Mr. and Mrs. Ruth were called to the police station.

"No one believes that George had a part in the break-in," the police captain said.

"But I want to warn you that if George stays around here, he'll end up in prison."

The suggestion was made that George be sent to St. Mary's Industrial School in Baltimore. It was a special school, run by the Roman Catholic Church, for boys with problems. Some were orphans, some were runaways. Some were from families too poor to support them. Others had police records.

There were usually 800 or more boys, age 7 to 21, living at St. Mary's. They were fed, clothed, given an education, and taught a trade.

Mr. and Mrs. Ruth agreed to send George to St. Mary's. It meant one less worry. So, early on the morning of June 13, 1902, seven-year-old George and his father took a trolley across the city to St. Mary's. There, with scarcely a good-bye, George's father left him.

The school's blocklike buildings were set

inside a high stone wall. The iron gates were kept locked, and the windows were covered with iron mesh. St. Mary's was known as "the Home." But to frightened George it looked more like a prison. Even the Catholic brothers who ran the school seemed like guards in their black clothes.

George was taken by one of the brothers to a dormitory with 200 iron beds, set up in rows. One bed had George's name on it. Under the bed was a small locker for his few belongings. He was given a blue shirt and a pair of overalls.

"Everybody wears overalls here," the brother said. "It's the school uniform."

George was then shown to a classroom. Since he had attended school so little, he was put in the first grade. He was so much bigger than his classmates he felt foolish. He had to sit up straight. He could speak only when he was told he could.

16

In the late afternoon school work ended. When the boys made a dash to the yard to play baseball, George hung back. He knew little or nothing about baseball.

A few of the boys were friendly, but most ignored him. Some pushed him around because he was new. At home, George would have used his fists. But he was afraid to fight here.

A baseball game in progress at St. Mary's

By suppertime he was very unhappy. He thought about trying to escape. But where would he go?

At bedtime, George marched with the others in his group to the dormitory. The boys put on nightshirts and knelt beside their beds. They joined in prayers under the watchful eye of a brother. George didn't know the prayers, but he moved his lips as if he did. Then he got into bed. Lights were out at eight o'clock.

George lay still, his muscles tight. The unhappiness that had been gathering inside him became worse. If there was only someone he could go to. But there never had been. His mother and his father didn't want him. Nobody did.

George knew he was going to cry no matter how hard he tried not to. He buried his face in the pillow so no one could hear.

He had no idea how long he had been

crying when he felt a hand on his shoulder. A brother was bending over the bed, one he had never seen before.

"Shhhh," the brother said. He put a finger to his lips. "Come with me, George. We'll have a talk."

George followed the brother to a small room.

"Sit down," the man said. "My name is Brother Matthias."

George stared at Brother Matthias. He was a big man, well over six feet.

"They told me you were coming to live with us, George," the brother said. "I'm glad." He smiled. He had a nice smile, and his eyes were blue.

"The first night is a hard one, George," he went on. "But don't worry. Things will work out." He was silent for a moment. "You've got a good build. You'll make a fine baseball player."

"I don't know much about it," George said.

"We'll see about that tomorrow," Brother Matthias said.

There was a small gas stove in the room. The brother made some hot chocolate. He gave George a big cupful. The chocolate tasted good.

"Drink up, young man," Brother Matthias said. "Then off to bed with you. And remember, if there's anything bothering you, come to me. We'll talk it over. Don't forget, George, I'm your friend."

3. Play Ball

The next afternoon Brother Matthias met George out on the playground. He had with him a baseball bat, a ball, and two gloves.

"George," he said. "You're about to discover the greatest sport of all—baseball."

And baseball it was for George from then on.

Brother Matthias taught George how to hold the bat and swing it. George batted, as he threw, left-handed. Soon he was hitting the ball at almost every try. Brother Matthias rounded up other young boys and started a pickup game.

Brother Matthias was physical director of St. Mary's as well as head of discipline. He was a very busy man. Even so he managed to coach George and the other young boys almost every afternoon. George began to have fun and to make friends.

At home George had always done pretty much as he wanted. It was different at St. Mary's. The boys got up at six sharp each morning. They dressed, then marched to chapel. Next came breakfast, followed by school at 7:30.

The brothers were strict. If their rules were not obeyed, swift punishment followed. Sometimes this meant standing in the yard during playtime, not speaking or being spoken to. The worst thing that could happen was to be forbidden to play baseball. There were other sports at the home, but baseball was *the* game. St. Mary's had more than 40 baseball teams.

In later years, George spoke of Brother
Matthias (above) as "the greatest man I ever
met."

George had been at the school about a month when Brother Matthias took him aside. "George," he said, "you're leaving St. Mary's."

George was startled. "What have I done wrong?" he asked.

"That's not it," Brother Matthias said. "Your mother has changed her mind. She wants you home. Your father's coming."

Back at the tavern, George's mother made a fuss over him. She said she had never meant to send him away. At first George missed the calm and order of St. Mary's. It was hard to get used to the noise of drunken fighting in the bar below. But before long George began going out with the street gang. He was soon in trouble again. His mother broke down in tears. She told her husband to put George back in St. Mary's.

So George went back, but a few weeks

later he was taken out again when his mother had another change of heart. From age seven until he was fifteen, George was put in St. Mary's and taken out four times. His fourth return home was a sad one. His mother, whose health had grown worse, died. After her death St. Mary's became George's only home.

George tried to act tough, as if what was happening didn't bother him. But inside he was hurt. The one person who seemed to understand what he was going through was Brother Matthias. To George, the brother was a father and his best friend.

"The greatest man I ever met," was the way he put it later.

Visiting day at the home was held one Sunday a month. Families and friends of the boys came calling. But as the months passed no one came to see George. To hide his disappointment, he made a joke of it.

"I haven't seen my father for so long," he once said with a laugh, "we'd have to be introduced."

George was always laughing and joking. He never let on, even to himself, how he really felt.

He played the big bass drum in the school band. Often he banged it so hard it drowned out the music. When somebody objected, George grinned and said, "You should thank me."

Everyone at St. Mary's liked George, most of all the little boys. Anybody who tried to bully one of them soon stopped if George found out. He remembered his first lonely days too well.

Like all of the boys at St. Mary's, George was taught a trade. He learned to be a shirtmaker. He once asked Brother Matthias if he thought he would make a good tailor.

"Of course you would, George," Brother

Matthias said. "But I think your career will be in baseball."

Brother Matthias had watched George advance over the years from baseball team to baseball team. George could hold down almost any position in the infield or outfield. Brother Matthias used him mainly as a catcher, although he was a good first baseman too. It wasn't until he was fifteen that George pitched in a game. Much to everybody's surprise, as well as his own, he struck out batter after batter.

By his eighteenth year George had become St. Mary's star pitcher. He was also the school's top hitter. Doubles and triples, as well as home runs, boomed off his bat.

When the students of Mount St. Joseph's, a Catholic college in Baltimore, heard about George, they bragged that they had a pitcher even better. A game was arranged between the first teams of the two schools.

St. Mary's winning baseball team. George is
standing near the flag at upper left.

The contest was held at St. Mary's on a
Saturday morning in September 1913. From
the first pitch George was in command. His
fast ball was a smoking bullet, his curve
unhittable. By the end of the game he had
struck out 22 Mount St. Joseph batters. He
had, himself, slugged in four runs, one of
them a homer. The game ended with Mount
St. Joseph shut out, 6-0.

After the game George was surprised to
learn that the brothers had invited a
special guest. He was Jack Dunn, owner

28

and manager of the famous professional baseball team, the Baltimore Orioles.

The Orioles at that time were in the International League. This league was not one of the two major leagues, the National and American. But it was the next best.

George was introduced to Mr. Dunn, who congratulated him on his playing. Nothing more was said. But five months later, shortly after George had turned nineteen, he was called into the school principal's office. With the principal were Brother Matthias and Jack Dunn.

"George," Brother Matthias said. "Mr. Dunn wants you to play baseball for the Orioles. He'll pay you $600 for the season."

George could scarcely believe his ears.

"He's giving me money to play baseball," George told a group of the boys afterward. "He's nuts. I would have done it for nothing."

4. The Tryout

On Friday, February 27, 1914, the heavy front gates of St. Mary's School were opened. George walked through. Behind him the pupils and staff of St. Mary's shouted good-bye. The last person to shake George's hand was Brother Matthias.

"You'll make it, George," the brother said.

"I'm sure going to try," George said. He was excited about starting his new life. Yet it was hard to leave St. Mary's. The school was the only real home he had ever known.

George met a number of Oriole players in downtown Baltimore. Together they traveled to the ball club's spring training camp in Fayetteville, North Carolina. Riding on a train for the first time was a thrill to George.

The players were put up in a hotel in town. When they went into the dining room for breakfast, George found to his delight that he could order anything on the menu. And the club would pay for it!

George was now 6 feet, 2 inches in height and weighed 180 pounds. He had a huge appetite. That morning he went through three stacks of wheatcakes. He had a double order of ham and eggs. He was about to start all over again when the team's trainer called out, "Time for practice."

George pushed back his plate. "Well," he said with a sigh. "I guess I've had enough." Then he added, "For now."

When the other players burst out laughing, George joined in. He was always able to see the funny side, even when the joke was on him.

The Orioles trained at the Fayetteville Fair Grounds. Daily workouts were held in batting, fielding, and pitching. Practice ended with a run around the horse track that circled the field. George was in top condition, and the running was easy for him. But some of the team's older players puffed and groaned as they tried to get into shape after a winter of soft living.

"Come on," George would yell as he sprinted past the veterans. "What are you old-timers waiting for—a wheelchair?"

George's kidding didn't sit well with the Oriole regulars. They made it clear that they wanted nothing to do with the rookie with the big mouth. They left George out of their card games and other social get-togethers. George was puzzled. At St. Mary's nobody minded being teased.

So George began making friends with the boys who came to watch the Orioles practice. It was always easy for George to get along with youngsters. The boys loaned him their bicycles whenever he felt like a ride.

The baseball practices became tougher as the training continued. Jack Dunn, the Orioles' owner-manager, had George work hard on his pitching. George had a good curve and a fast ball. He could hit too. Even the old-timers blinked when George's bat connected.

"Ruth is the most promising young ball player I've ever seen," Dunn told reporters.

Jack Dunn was so interested in his rookie that the other ballplayers began to refer to George as "Dunn's babe." Before very long everybody was calling George, "Babe." From then on George Ruth was Babe Ruth.

Toward the end of the training period, Jack Dunn put up a list of the players who would stay with the Orioles. No one was surprised to see Babe Ruth's name on it.

When the season opened, Dunn had Babe pitch the Orioles' second game. Much to Babe's delight, he won it, shutting out Buffalo, 6-0. The victory was the start of a string of wins for Babe, at home and on the road.

By the end of his first road trip, Babe was no longer a rookie. He was a seasoned professional. The Oriole veterans now welcomed him as one of their own.

Jack Dunn was so pleased with Babe's showing that he increased his season's pay from $600 to $1,200, then to $1,800. The flood of money dazzled Babe.

Babe went to the new motion picture shows. He ate big delicious meals. He sent boxes of candy and other treats to the boys at St. Mary's.

Thanks in part to Babe Ruth, the

Baltimore Orioles became the best team in the league. But their owner, Jack Dunn, was in money trouble. A third major baseball league, called the Federal League, had just been formed. This new league had a team in Baltimore named the Terrapins. Baltimore fans began to turn out to watch the Terrapins instead of going to Oriole games. As a result Jack Dunn made very little money from at-home contests.

One day in July he called Babe into his office. "Babe," he said, "I'm in such a jam for cash I've got to do something I don't want to do. I'm selling eight of my best players. Three are going to the Boston Red Sox. You're one of them."

"Me?" Babe exclaimed. "To the Red Sox!" He couldn't believe it. The Boston club was one of the greatest in the major leagues. The Sox had won the first World Series in 1903. They'd won again in 1912.

"I hate to lose you, Babe," Jack Dunn said. "But it will be your gain. Just think, in less than half a season of pro ball, you'll be in the big time."

Babe ran his hand through his thick black hair. "Yeah," he said. "The big time!"

He'd be sorry to leave the Orioles and the man who had given him his chance. It had been Mr. Dunn who had turned him from a schoolboy pitcher into a real pro.

But the Boston Red Sox!

5. The Majors

Babe Ruth was one of the first passengers off the train when it pulled into Boston on the morning of July 11, 1914. He reported right away to Bill Carrigan, the Red Sox manager. Carrigan lost little time. He had Babe pitch that very afternoon against the Cleveland Indians. Babe won the game, 4-3. He was overjoyed.

"This is going to be a cinch," Babe announced loudly to everybody in the locker room after the game. He didn't mean to sound big-headed. He was just eager and happy. It was his nature to come out and say whatever crossed his mind.

Babe's powerful left arm made him a star pitcher for the Boston Red Sox.

But Babe soon found out that it wasn't all that easy in the major leagues. Carrigan used him on the mound again five days later against the Detroit Tigers. Babe breezed along fine for five innings. Then the Tiger bats began hitting. Babe was driven out of the game. The Tigers won.

Babe was more puzzled than downcast. "It's funny," he said to Carrigan. "I had the feeling that those Detroit batters knew what pitch was coming almost before I threw it."

A few days later, Babe was at pitching practice when the manager called him to the bench.

"I've been watching you, Babe," Carrigan said. "You're telegraphing your pitches. No wonder you were knocked out of the box the other day."

"Telegraphing?" Babe said. "How?"

"Every time you throw a curve, you stick

the tip of your tongue out of the corner of your mouth," Carrigan said. "Somebody on the Tigers likely got wise and spread the word."

"Well, I'll be," Babe said. "I didn't know I was doing that."

"Better cure yourself fast, son," Carrigan said, "or you won't last in this man's league."

Babe worked hard throwing curves. Soon he felt he had got over the habit of showing his tongue. He expected Carrigan would now use him. But the team's experienced pitchers were coming up with wins. So Carrigan let Babe sit on the bench as game after game went by.

In August Babe was told that he was being sent back to the minors. He was to play with the Providence Grays of the International League. The owner of the Boston Red Sox had bought the Grays. They were in a tight battle for the lead in the league. They needed pitching help.

The news of the move upset Babe. As a small boy he had been badly hurt when his father and mother had sent him away. Now he felt it was happening again. Carrigan and the Red Sox didn't want him.

Well, he'd go to Providence. But he was determined to get back to the big league soon.

Babe's stay with the Providence Grays turned out to be one of the best things that ever happened to him. The Grays' manager, Bill Donovan, had been a top major-league pitcher. Impressed by Babe's throwing ability, Donovan began coaching him. Babe pitched twelve games for the Grays and won nine of them.

Babe needed no help when it came to batting. "I think I was born as a hitter," he once said.

Even so, Babe felt that he wasn't making full use of his power at the plate. While at Providence he began trying out new ways of batting. He found that he could get the most out of his full swing by gripping his heavy bat at the very end of the handle. Then, with his feet planted close together in the batter's box, he'd wait for the pitch, his body twisted around so that part of his back was toward the pitcher.

If he decided to swing at the pitched ball, he'd take a full step forward with his right foot and bring his bat lashing around. He swung from the heels. Babe wasn't interested in placement hitting. It was all or nothing. When his bat connected, the ball was struck with a vicious uppercut and blasted high and far.

During his stay with Providence, Babe had a batting average of .300. What pleased him most took place in a game against the Maple Leafs in Toronto, Canada, on September 5, 1914. Babe slammed the ball out of the park for his first home run in an official professional baseball game.

When the International League season ended, the Providence Grays were champions. Much of the credit was given to young Babe Ruth.

Late in September he was called back to Boston. The Red Sox had just a few games left to play. Carrigan sent Babe in to pitch one of them. He won it.

Carrigan slapped him on the back. "Nice going," he said. "Welcome back."

Welcome back. They were great words to hear. But perhaps even better words came in a letter a few days later. It was from Brother Matthias and said, "You're doing fine, George. I'm proud of you."

6. First Season

Babe Ruth had a girl friend in Boston, named Helen Woodford. She was dark-haired and pretty, and she worked as a waitress in a coffee shop where Babe often ate breakfast. Babe and Helen fell in love and were married on October 17, 1914.

They went to Baltimore on their honeymoon. There Babe looked up his father. Babe wanted to forgive the past. Mr. Ruth invited Helen and Babe to spend the winter in the rooms over the tavern.

The Red Sox club was paying Babe $3,500 a year, a good salary for those times. With plenty of money to spend, Babe and Helen had a carefree winter. Several times Babe visited St. Mary's, where he always got a big welcome.

When spring training began Babe was one of the first to report. He worked hard and was in top shape when the 1915 season opened. He pitched two early Red Sox games, winning the first, losing the second. Then came his third on May 6, 1915. It was one he would never forget.

The game was against the New York Yankees. At that time the Yankee Stadium had not been built. The Yankees used the New York Giants' Polo Grounds for home games.

The Yankee pitcher that day was a right-hander named Jack Warhop. The first innings were scoreless. Babe was the lead-off batter for Boston in the third. He took a called first strike.

Then, as he later wrote, "Warhop threw me an underhand delivery and I put a little fire behind it and knocked it into the right field stands." He had hit his first major-league home run.

The Red Sox manager knew that Babe had the makings of a great pitcher. But Carrigan was bothered by Babe's spells of wild throwing. He began spending more and more time with his big left-hander, working on his control. After a while Babe settled down. By the end of the 1915 season, he had won 18 games and lost 8. He had done well in batting, too, with an average of .315. Babe had slammed out a total of four home runs—twice as many as any other Red Sox that year.

Best of all, the Red Sox had won the American League pennant. They were in the World Series against the Philadelphia Phillies.

From the beginning, Babe was an outstanding slugger. He is fourth from left in the front row of this Red Sox team picture.

"My first full season in the majors," Babe said gleefully to Helen, "and I'll be pitching in a World Series."

But Babe was in for a big disappointment. Carrigan felt that Babe wasn't quite ready to stand up to the strain of World Series pitching. He called on his veterans.

The Boston Red Sox won the championship. Babe's only appearance was as a pinch-hitter in the first game. He grounded out.

"I ate my heart out on the bench," Babe remembered.

The following season of 1916 was a good one for Babe. He won 23 games and lost 12. Even though his batting average of .272 wasn't up to the previous year, he had three home runs.

Again Boston was in a World Series, this time against the Brooklyn Dodgers.

"Now do I get to pitch?" Babe asked Carrigan.

The Red Sox manager grinned. "If I didn't let you pitch in this series, Babe," he said, "the Boston fans would string me up. The second game is yours."

The Red Sox defeated Brooklyn in the opener. Then came the second game.

More than 40,000 noisy fans packed the Boston ball park on Monday afternoon, October 9, 1916. Each team scored a single run early in the game. Then both Babe and the Dodger pitcher settled down. The scoreboard read 1-1, inning after inning. By the end of the ninth there was still a deadlock. The tenth, eleventh, twelfth, and thirteenth innings passed with no change. The sun set. In those days baseball parks were not lighted. Darkness began to close in. The excitement in the stands and on the field mounted with each out.

In the top of the fourteenth inning, Babe got the Dodgers out with no score. The Red

Sox came to bat. The first Boston batter was walked. A sacrifice fly sent him to second. The next Red Sox batter slammed out a solid two-base hit. The runner came racing in from second to score the tie-breaking run.

Babe had won his first World Series game, 2-1. Not only that, he had pitched the longest game in World Series history.

The Red Sox continued on to capture the world championship, four games to one. Babe had no chance to pitch a second game. But that didn't matter. Now he really belonged with the champions.

7. The Wild One

In the fall of 1916, Bill Carrigan retired as manager of the Red Sox. Babe hated to see him go. Carrigan had been like a father to him.

The following April, the United States became involved in World War I, then raging in Europe. As all young men were subject to military service, there was talk that professional baseball might be stopped.

Babe wasn't required to serve because he was married. But he joined the National Guard and stood ready to do his part. His unit was never called up. And major-league baseball kept on being played.

Babe (second from right) was a mainstay of the Red Sox pitching staff.

When the 1917 season opened, Babe got off to a fast start. He won the first eight games he pitched. He was just as busy with his bat, cracking out hits.

Babe was friendly and easygoing off the diamond. But on it he was tough and played to win. Without Carrigan around to calm him down, Babe often lost his temper and argued with umpires. Once he came storming off the mound when the plate umpire called one of his pitches a ball.

Babe rushed up to the official. "You're blind as a bat!" he yelled. "That was a strike!"

The umpire wasn't taking any such talk. "Get out there and pitch, Ruth," he said. "Or you're through."

Some said Babe swung his fist at the umpire. Others claimed Babe pushed him. In any case Babe was put out of the game. He wasn't allowed to play for ten days. He was also fined $100. Babe later said what he'd done was stupid.

In spite of such flare-ups, Babe had a good year. He finished with 24 games won against 14 lost. His batting average was a high .325. That included two home runs.

Babe's success and the money it brought him began to go to his head. His salary had been raised from $3,500 to $5,000 in

1917. It was increased to $7,000 in 1918. Babe had also received almost $8,000 as his share in the two World Series victories. At that time the dollar was worth four to five times what it is today.

Carrigan had seen to it that Babe didn't throw his money away. But now that there was nobody to stop him, Babe spent the dollars fast. He went to cocktail parties and often stayed out drinking until daybreak. This was strictly against training rules. So was his overeating.

Sometimes Babe had nine or ten meals a day. He put on weight, going over 215 pounds. Stories were told of his huge appetite.

"I saw the Babe having dinner," one fan reported. "He polished off a whole roast chicken—himself. With potatoes, peas, corn, the works. And two pitchers of beer. On top of everything, he ate a whole custard pie."

In 1916 the Red Sox had a new manager named Ed Barrow. He didn't like the way Babe was acting. He tried hard to reason with him. When that didn't work, Barrow threatened to fine Babe. Babe always promised to do better. He would for a while. Then he'd slip back to his old ways.

Babe's wild life seemed to have no bad effect on his playing. He kept on pitching winning games. But it was his hitting that made headlines. In 1918 Babe knocked out eleven home runs before June 30. People began flocking to the ball parks whenever and wherever he played. The fans found Babe exciting even when he struck out. The force of his powerful swing whirled his big body around like a top. Sometimes when he missed the ball, he was thrown off his feet.

Like the other Red Sox pitchers, Babe played every fourth or fifth day. That was so he could rest his pitching arm between games. As a result the Red Sox missed his run-getting bat on his resting days.

Manager Ed Barrow had been thinking about this, and one afternoon he talked to Babe.

"Babe," he said. "How would you like to see a little action on the days you aren't pitching?"

"Would I!" Babe exclaimed. "Can a duck swim?"

"Well, you might take a turn at first base," Barrow said. "Or play the outfield. That would give you extra times at bat."

"Sounds great," Babe said. Batting was what he liked to do best.

From then on Babe was in the Red Sox lineup every day. When he wasn't pitching he sometimes played first base, but mostly left field. Barrow put him fourth in the batting order, in the cleanup spot. By the end of the season, Babe had 95 hits for an average of .300. His home run total remained at 11.

Late in August Babe had tragic news. His father had been killed in a fist fight. Babe and Helen went to the funeral.

That season the Red Sox once again ended as pennant winners. Babe pitched the opening game of the World Series against the Chicago Cubs. He won it, 1-0. In so doing Babe added nine scoreless World Series innings to the thirteen he had pitched in the 1916 Series.

Babe took the mound again for the fourth game. He blanked the Cubs for 7$\frac{2}{3}$ innings before giving up a run. He won the game, 3-2. He now had set a World Series record by pitching 29$\frac{2}{3}$ scoreless innings in a row. The record stood for 42 years. It was finally broken by Whitey Ford of the Yankees in 1961. Ford pitched 32 consecutive scoreless innings.

The Red Sox won the 1918 World Series, four games to two.

Even before the 1919 season opened, Babe made news. In an exhibition game during spring training in Florida, Babe banged out what has been called the longest home run ever hit.

Sportswriters on the scene ran over to measure the distance the ball had traveled.

"I make it 550 feet," one reporter said.

"It went 600 easy," another said. "I measured it with a tape."

The exact distance was not officially recorded. But one thing was clear. Babe Ruth had never hit a longer home run—nor had anybody else.

On the way north after spring training, the Red Sox played many exhibition games. Now that World War I was over, more and more people turned out to watch baseball. One of the exhibition games was held in

Baltimore. Babe saw to it that Brother Matthias and a group of St. Mary's boys had seats. That afternoon Babe came to bat six times. Twice he was walked. The other four times he hit home runs.

"How could I miss," he said, "with St. Mary's watching me?"

After the game the boys and Brother Matthias met with Babe. Babe enjoyed the reunion until Brother Matthias took him aside.

"I told you you'd make it, George," Brother Matthias said. "And you have. But you've failed in one thing."

"What's that, brother?" Babe asked.

"In the way you've been behaving," Brother Matthias said. "Now you listen to me, young man. You straighten up!"

Babe hung his head the way he had as a small boy at St. Mary's when he was in trouble. "I'll try, brother," he said.

The 1919 season had barely got underway when it became clear that it was going to be a Babe Ruth year. He was now earning $10,000 annually. Ed Barrow still had him pitching, but Babe was being used more and more in the outfield. By July 1, Babe had knocked out 7 home runs. By midsummer the number jumped to 15, then to 20. The most home runs ever hit by a big-league player in a single year was 27, back in 1884. Fans everywhere now began rooting for Babe to beat the record.

He didn't disappoint them. On September 20, he got his 27th four-bagger, tying the record. A few days later, in New York, he drilled out his 28th. Then, late in September, Babe hit his final home run of the year. It was his 29th.

Experts said no one, not even Babe Ruth himself, would ever equal that number again. Pictures of Babe's big round face

60

with its flat nose and black button eyes grinned out of papers across the country. The fact that the Red Sox failed to win the pennant didn't bother the Boston fans. They had Babe Ruth.

A Babe Ruth Day was held at Boston's Fenway Park. Speeches were made. The band played. Babe was given a diamond ring and other presents as the crowd cheered.

Then, some weeks later came the shattering news. Babe Ruth would not be playing for the Red Sox in 1920.

Boston's great star had been sold to the New York Yankees.

8. The Big Town

The news sent shock waves through Boston. "It's a joke," fans said. "The Sox would never let the Babe go."

But it was no joke. The details came out in the newspapers. The Red Sox owner was in need of money. The two owners of the New York Yankees had plenty. So a deal was made. Babe Ruth's contract was sold for $100,000 cash. He became the property of New York. As for Babe himself, the Yankees doubled his pay to $20,000. No ballplayer had ever earned that much before.

Babe began his first season as a Yankee by hitting the ball even harder than the year before. By June 1, 1920, he had 12 home runs. By July 25, he had 29, tying his 1919 record. Miller Huggins, the little Yankee manager, had no thought of using Babe as a pitcher. Huggins had him in the outfield every day and batting fourth. He later moved Babe to third in the batting order.

Babe and his big hitting had brought a big change to baseball. No longer was the

The Yankees' star batter hits his twenty-first home run of the 1920 season.

pitcher the game's idol. The spotlight was on the batsman. Other players began to copy Babe's full swing. The number of extra-base hits mounted.

A new kind of ball that aided the long hitter was now being used. Its stronger yarn was wound tighter around the core of the ball. As a result the new baseball was harder and had more bounce. The "lively" or "rabbit" ball, as it was called, could be hit farther.

By the end of the 1920 season, Babe had pounded the lively ball for 54 home runs. His batting average soared to .376.

Sportswriters began to give Babe such names as the Sultan of Swat, the King of Clout, the Prince of Pounders. He was also called the Bambino, the Italian name for baby. Everything about Babe made news, even his clothes. He could be spotted anywhere by his camel's hair polo coat and cap.

Crowds of boys gathered around him wherever he went. Babe always welcomed them. After a ball game the other players would hurry off to the showers. Babe usually stayed on the field to talk to the "keeds," as he called them.

"Keeds like me," he once said. "And I like them."

Babe would always go out of his way to help a child. There was a story about an eleven-year-old boy from New Jersey, named Johnny Sylvester, who had undergone a serious operation. The operation was successful, but Johnny seemed to lose all his desire to get well. Johnny's father knew that his son's hero was Babe Ruth. So he asked Babe if he would send Johnny an autographed baseball in the hope that it would cheer him up. Instead of mailing the ball to Johnny, Babe went to see him one morning.

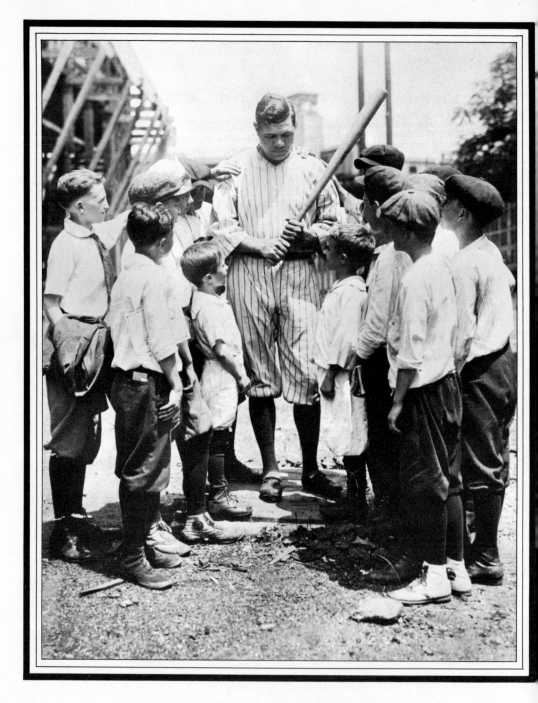

The Sultan of Swat was the hero of a whole
generation of small boys. He is surrounded
here by some of his adoring fans.

"Hello, keed," Babe said when he walked into Johnny's room.

Johnny was so surprised that he couldn't speak.

Babe sat down beside the bed, and before long Johnny was asking questions a mile a minute. Finally Babe stood up.

"I'd better be moving along," he said. "My manager would get me if I turned up late for the game this afternoon."

Babe shook hands with Johnny. "Tell you what," Babe said. "If you promise to do your best to get well, I'll do something for you."

"What?" Johnny asked.

"I'll hit a home run for you this afternoon," Babe said.

Babe did hit a home run that afternoon, and Johnny did improve and get well.

Babe's interest in children came from his days at St. Mary's. He was shocked when a fire destroyed a number of the school buildings. And when he heard that the brothers were trying to raise money to rebuild, Babe sent a letter to Brother Matthias.

"Get the school band together," Babe wrote. "It's going traveling. So are you. I have a plan."

Babe arranged to have the St. Mary's band travel with the Yankee team on a road trip. The band played at the ball parks before the games, and collections were taken up. There were also fund-raising banquets with Babe as the main speaker. More than $10,000 was raised for St. Mary's.

Later on Helen and Babe adopted a baby girl. Her name was Dorothy. Having a daughter quieted Babe down. The three of them spent the off-season on the 80-acre farm Babe had bought outside Boston.

Babe outdid himself in 1921. His batting average was .378, and his home-run count

Dorothy and her famous father at the ball park

went to 59. For the first time the Yankees won the American League pennant.

Everyone thought the Yankees would win when they met the New York Giants in the World Series. But it wasn't to be. Babe injured his left elbow early in the Series. He did manage to hit his first World Series home run in the fourth game, but it wasn't enough. The Giants won the championship, five games to three.

Babe was aware of his value to the Yankee owners. When it came time to talk about his 1922 contract, he was ready. Colonel Huston, then coowner of the club with Colonel Ruppert, offered Babe $40,000. When Babe turned it down, the amount was raised to $50,000.

"I tell you what, Colonel," Babe said. "I'll sign if you make it $52,000 yearly."

The matter of $2,000 more didn't mean much to the Yankee owner. But Colonel Huston was curious to know why Babe wanted that amount.

"Well," Babe said when he was asked to explain. "When I was a kid I used to dream of making a thousand bucks a week. And there are 52 weeks in a year."

Babe got his huge salary.

9. The House That Ruth Built

In spite of Brother Matthias's advice to "straighten up," Babe went back to his old wild ways. He bought the raciest cars and drove them fast. When he wrecked one, he bought another.

He was overeating and drinking again and staying up all night. Often he'd come tearing into the ball park late for the game, not having been to bed. Miller Huggins, the Yankee manager, did his best to check Babe's wildness, but with no real success.

The year 1922 turned out to be a terrible one for Babe. His home-run total dipped to

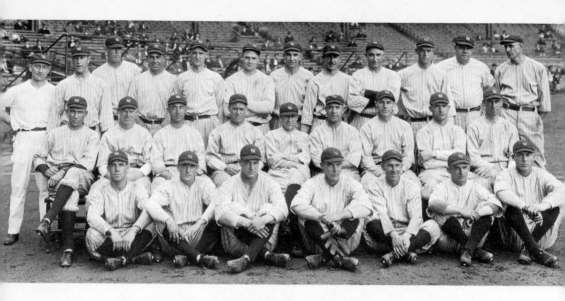

The incredible Yankees in 1923. Babe Ruth
stands second from right in the back row.

The Babe and Bob Meusel, two
great Yankee players

Waite Hoyt and Babe Ruth, with
Manager Miller Huggins

a low 35. The Yankees managed to win the pennant, but they lost the World Series again to the Giants in four straight games.

Reporters were critical of Babe. So were the fans. Instead of cheers, Babe began getting boos. He didn't seem to care. All he thought of was food and drink and the next party.

By this time Babe had hired a business manager to look after his affairs. The business manager was worried. If Babe couldn't be made to realize what he was doing, his career might soon be over.

The business manager got an idea. He arranged for a dinner to be held for sportswriters and well-known New Yorkers. Babe was to be the honored guest.

At the dinner, when reporters began to question Babe about the way he was behaving, he lost his temper. He answered them angrily. Then one of the banquet speakers stood up. He was State Senator Jimmy Walker, later mayor of New York.

"Babe Ruth," he said, "you are making a bigger salary than anyone ever received as a ball player. But the bigger the salary, the bigger fool you have become."

Babe could scarcely believe what he heard. Jimmy Walker was his friend.

"The kids of America think of you as their hero," Senator Walker went on. "They look up to you, worship you. And then what happens? You carouse and abuse your great body. It is exactly as though Santa Claus himself suddenly were to take off his beard to reveal the features of a villain. The kids have seen their idol shattered and their dreams broken."

The anger that had reddened Babe's face now was gone. He looked down at the floor and squeezed his big hands together.

"If we didn't love you, Babe," Jimmy

Walker said, "I wouldn't tell you these things. . . . Will you not, for the kids of America, promise to mend your ways? Will you not give back to those kids their great idol?"

Babe's eyes were full of tears. "So help me, Jim," he said, "I will. I'll go back to my farm and get in shape."

Babe did just that. He gave up drinking and partying. He went on a diet. He exercised hard. When the 1923 season opened, he was in fine condition.

The Yankees' first game in 1923 would celebrate the opening of their new ball park, Yankee Stadium, the largest and the most modern in America. It was called the "House That Ruth Built" because so many fans had paid their money to see Babe play.

The Yankees' opponent in the opening game was Babe's old club, the Boston Red

Sox. Long before starting time on April 18, the new triple-decked grandstand was filled. So were the outfield bleachers.

When the Yankees came to bat in the third inning, they were in the lead, 1-0. Two Yankees got on base. Then as Babe Ruth stepped up to take his position at home plate, an amazing thing happened. The *New York Times* records that, "The biggest crowd in baseball history rose to its feet and let loose the biggest shout in baseball history." It was in tribute to Babe Ruth.

Standing there at home plate, Babe Ruth looked out at the sea of faces. Here he was, the boy nobody had wanted, being honored as few had been before. If only his mother and his father could have been there.

Babe's hands tightened around the handle of his bat. He knew he had disappointed

76

At the grand opening of Yankee Stadium, Babe hit the first home run ever recorded there. Below, an early view of the stadium.

not just the youngsters but thousands of other fans. Now it was up to him to show them that he had really come back.

Babe let the Red Sox pitcher get the count up to two balls, two strikes. Then, on the next throw, Babe brought the bat around with all his strength.

The bat met the ball squarely. It became a white blur high above the playing field and ended its flight ten rows deep in the bleachers. It was the first home run ever hit in Yankee Stadium.

The Yankees won the ball game, 4-1. And Babe Ruth was back at the top, where he belonged.

By the end of the 1923 season, Babe had hit 41 home runs. His batting average was .393, the highest of his career. Best of all, he won the American Leagues' Most Valuable Player award.

As pennant winners, the Yankees met the

Giants in still another World Series. This time the Yankees were victorious, four games to two. Babe walloped three homers, two in one game. It was the Yankees' first world championship.

Babe remained in top form through the next season, finishing up with a batting average of .378 and 46 homers. It was more than enough to give him the batting championship.

Then in 1925 everything seemed to go wrong for Babe. He put it best when he wrote, "I changed from the batting champ of 1924 to the big bust of 1925."

His marriage to Helen had broken up. Over the years they had drifted apart. Babe quarreled with the Yankee manager and was later fined. To add to his woes, Babe was struck down with what was called "the bellyache heard round the world," because it caused so much comment. The severe illness that put Babe in the hospital was first thought to have come from the stuffing down of endless hot dogs and soda pop. Actually Babe had an intestinal abscess which required an operation.

As a result, Babe was late getting into action that year. He hit only 25 homers in 1925.

The 1926 season proved more favorable. Babe came up with 47 home runs, and the Yankees won the pennant. In the World Series against the St. Louis Cardinals, Babe was sensational. He knocked in four home runs, three in one game. It was an amazing feat never done before. Even so, the Cardinals won the Series, four games to three.

10. The Final Out

The 1927 New York Yankees have been called the greatest baseball team of all time. Aside from Babe Ruth, the Yankees had other big hitters. They had the young Columbia University star, Lou Gehrig, at first base; Tony Lazzeri, at second; and Bob Meusel and Earle Combs in the outfield with Babe.

There was never any doubt that the Yankees would win the pennant that season. What the fans were interested in was a home-run race between Lou Gehrig and Babe. Each one was knocking out four-baggers at a rapid clip. Babe wanted to

Between seasons, "Larrupin' Lou" Gehrig and the Babe went on tour. Their antics endeared them to the fans.

break his own record of 59, set in 1921. Lou was out to give the champ a run for his money.

Through the early summer the home-run derby remained close. On August 10, Gehrig was ahead with 38 homers to Babe's 36. A week later they were even. By the end of the month, Babe had surged into the lead with 43 to Lou's 40.

From then on it was all Babe. He hit his 50th on September 11, his 55th on the 21st. On September 29th, Babe hit two big ones in one game, his 58th and 59th. Now he was even with his own record. Would he be able to top it?

The next to the last game of the season was played on September 30, between the Yankees and the Washington Senators. If Babe was to break his record, he had to do it right away.

That afternoon the Yankee Stadium was

The mighty Babe scores in the 1927 series.

jammed with fans who had come to cheer the great Babe on. The first time up Babe was walked.

"Let him hit!" an angry fan screamed at the Washington pitcher.

The next two times at bat Babe swung hard, but in each case had to settle for a single. The crowd was now getting anxious.

In the eighth inning Babe had his last

84

chance. As he left the dugout Miller
Huggins said, "You can do it, big boy."

"I'm going to, Hug," Babe said.

Babe waited out the pitcher. The count
was one ball, one strike when Babe leaned
into the next delivery. The ball was blasted
into the right-field bleachers.

Babe had scarcely rounded first base
when the spectators were on their feet. A
thunder of cheering greeted the heavyset

Yankee star as he ran on. Babe held his cap high in the air.

Sixty home runs in one year. It was a record Babe would never beat, nor would anyone else in a 154-game season. Roger Maris of the Yankees clouted 61 home runs in 1961 but in a season of 162 games.

The 1927 World Series was a runaway for the Yankees. They knocked off the Pittsburgh Pirates in four straight games, with Babe hitting a homer in the third game and another in the fourth. The Bronx Bombers, as the Yankees were now being called, were on top of the baseball world.

The Yankees kept on going for more of the same in 1928. Babe got himself 54 home runs during the season. And he led his team to victory over the St. Louis Cardinals in the 1928 World Series, four games to none. Babe cracked out three homers.

Babe and his wife, Helen, had now been

separated for many years. In January 1929, Babe was shocked when word came that Helen had died in a fire in her Boston home. He left at once to attend the funeral.

During the time that Babe and Helen had been apart, Babe had fallen in love with a beautiful widow, Claire Hodgson. Babe and Claire were married in the spring of 1929. Babe's adopted daughter, Dorothy, now aged nine, lived with them in New York. And so did Julie, Claire's thirteen-year-old daughter by her first marriage.

Babe's marriage to Claire was one of the best things that ever happened to him. She was loyal, steady, and levelheaded. She brought a calmness to Babe's life he had never known before. At last he began to save money and to take care of himself.

In 1929 the Yankees began putting numbers on the backs of their players' uniforms so the fans could identify each player. The custom later spread through the major leagues. The Yankee numbers were given out according to the batting order. Babe Ruth got number 3. His home-run hitting rival, Lou Gehrig, who batted next, received number 4.

The rivalry between Babe and Lou led to some bad feeling between them. This was later patched up, and they became good

Babe still showed traces of genius as he slid into home plate in a 1934 game.

friends. Next to Babe, Lou Gehrig was one of the greatest Yankee players of that period. He was known as the Iron Horse because he played in a record 2,130 league games without an interrruption.

Babe's salary had now risen to $70,000 a year. By 1930 it went to $80,000. He was being paid more money than Herbert Hoover, then president of the United States. When this was pointed out to Babe, a big grin spread over his face. "Why not?" he said. "I had a better year than he did."

But Babe's best years were coming to a close. His home-run totals began to decline. In 1930 he had 49; in 1931, he had 46. In 1932, the year of his "called-shot" homer, he hit 41. The count dropped to 34 in 1933.

In that year, the first All-Star game was played in Chicago. Babe came through as he always had. In the third inning, he powered a two-run homer.

By 1934 age was slowing Babe down. He was now 39, old for an athlete. His home run total skidded to 22. His batting average was .288. His pay had dropped, too, to $35,000. He played in only 125 games.

Babe's last year with the Yankees was 1934. He played his final games for the New York club in Washington, D.C. He wanted more than anything to come up with a home run. Instead, he went hitless.

Yet to Babe the afternoon was rewarding, for the St. Mary's school band had traveled from Baltimore to blare out a farewell to their great hero. Babe's eyes were misty as he shook each boy by the hand. There was just one thing wrong. Brother Matthias was not there. He had died the previous year.

Babe had hoped to end his baseball career managing the New York Yankees or one of the other major-league clubs. But this was not to be.

An aging Babe Ruth slugs one for the Braves.

"You had such a hard time managing yourself," he was told. "How can you expect to manage others?"

Babe did take a position in 1935 with the Boston Braves of the National League. He was to act as an assistant manager and play the outfield on occasions. His stay was brief. But before he left baseball for good, Babe put on one last amazing batting display.

On May 25, 1935, with the Braves playing the Pirates in Pittsburgh, Babe became the

At the twenty-fifth anniversary of the
"House That Ruth Built," Babe said a last
good-bye to the New York Yankees.

home-run king of old. He hit three gigantic home runs. One of them rocketed clear out of the ball park.

In November 1946 the great slugger became ill. He was taken to the hospital, where he was operated on for cancer of the throat. His recovery was slow and far from complete. He did, however, manage to put in an appearance at Yankee Stadium on Sunday, April 27, 1947. This was a special day named by the commissioner of baseball as Babe Ruth Day. It was celebrated in every major-league ball park.

Before the packed stands in Yankee Stadium and with members of the current Yankee team lined up, Babe Ruth said his good-bye. He was no longer the barrel-chested six-footer. He had lost much weight. His face was lined and his once black hair streaked with white.

"The only real game is baseball," Babe

told the crowd. His voice was husky and weak. "You've got to start from the bottom when you're six or seven years old. You've got to let it grow up with you." He paused, then he said, "There have been so many lovely things said about me, I'm glad I had the opportunity to thank everybody. Thank you."

Babe had been one of the five original players elected to baseball's Hall of Fame in 1936. Now he donated his number 3 uniform, his glove, his shoes, and the bat he had used to hit his 60th home run. They were all put on permanent display in the Baseball Hall of Fame at Cooperstown, New York. The Yankees retired Babe's number 3. It would never be used again.

When Babe felt well enough, he played golf, a game he had come to like. He also did some traveling around the country to interest people in junior baseball. During this period he began what was called the Babe Ruth Foundation. Its purpose was to help needy children get an education through scholarships and prizes.

Babe's traveling stopped when he became ill again. He gradually grew worse. Then, on August 16, 1948, Babe died. He was 53.

Babe Ruth was honored throughout the land and the world. His body lay in state in Yankee Stadium, the House That Ruth Built. Lines of people filed past. He had become more than a great baseball player. He had become a legend.

In time many of Babe Ruth's major-league records were broken. Henry Aaron, playing for the Atlanta Braves, passed Babe's lifetime total of 714 home runs in 1974. But lettered on the bronze tablet at Cooperstown honoring Babe is a record that can never be topped. He was *the greatest drawing card in the history of baseball.*